Stir Thoughts but Don't Spill the Tea

Thea Panes- Demetillo

Stir Thoughts but Don't Spill the Tea
Philippine Copyright © 2024 by Thea Panes-Demetillo

Published by Thea Panes-Demetillo
Taguig City, Metro Manila
theapdemetillo@gmail.com

Cover design by Marco Luis Bartolo
Interior design by Alvin Demetillo
Images for page breakers were all AI-generated.
ISBN 978-621-06-1972-0

All musings contained in this book are personal to the author and do not have anything to do with her full-time profession. They do not represent any of her organizations, past or present.

If you arm yourself with honesty, you become your greatest fan and worst critic at the same time.

Never yield that power to someone else.

— TPD

Introduction

A couple of years and a few juvenile dreams back, I said I would write a book as a retirement project. My career is still in full swing, and I'm a few months shy of turning 50, but I finally decided to fan this flame rather than wait for that dream to happen. Right this very moment, you are going through pages of a book that don't carry any weight of historical events or political affluence or don't camouflage hues of a fictional bestseller. In this book, you are given full access to what used to be private thoughts — some of which will hopefully resonate with you or trigger a whole new set of realizations. As you rummage through these words and spaces in between, please know that often, answers to our questions are neither in the classroom, the next board meeting, nor in a post shared by an influencer. That journey is always personal as it always has been for me.

In an era where there is so much fake news and clickbait, "spilling the tea" has piqued the interest of both viewers and readers. As a result, social media platforms have become a goldmine of marketing ploys for advertising mileage. Sadly, not everything we read or watch is true. This book won't spew any of that. In fact, it aims to snap you out of that whole conundrum for some intimate time between my musings, crawling page by page like a vine to entangle with yours. It's when we fully immerse ourselves in those reflective moments that we get to experience what I love to call as "loud quiet" — when there are no words said and heard; no chance for a banter but there is an imposing flow of thoughts marshaled in silence to find their place vis-a-vis personal experiences. I am publishing them here (as talking to myself is getting too weird) without the ugly and distasteful elements of revealing secrets, sources and even stories shared with me in confidence. If I get lucky though, sharing this book with you might come at a time where we are both "just wanting to make sense of something." Whether it's a curveball thrown your way, a relationship you didn't think would end, or a promotion that didn't happen, they create this dissonance that is so arduous to pacify. Sometimes, our only ally is a moment: perhaps five minutes of solitude, where we are allowed to "process" a population of emotions with a purposeful intent to get through the day or move on for good. I also would like to propose bringing the best "companion" during these moments because the best musings come with a side of tea — and maybe a biscuit.

These musings that cross our minds like a lost stranger trying to find her way or one that takes permanent residence in our thoughts often "see the light of day" in conversations with a best friend over a good cup of tea. My partiality to tea, in this case, is intentional, as I am not a coffee drinker and have found that my preference would exclusively hop on a carousel of tea flavors depending on the time of day or even the mood of the moment. These reflections are also probably not the kind we would verbally peel off with someone prone to judge us because these thoughts are associated with character. Whether we admit it or not, no one wants their character assassinated. You know that your level of maturity has exceeded the peaks of Mount-I-Should-Know-Better when you choose to embrace them anyway — because they are the heart, mind, and soul that make who you really are. No matter what we say or do, someone out there is going to judge — and that is okay. People you choose to matter to you are equipped with the right amount of understanding to love you.

I chose to publish these musings with the intent of introducing the art of "MUSEcasting." When I was thinking of a theme for my book, I didn't have to emancipate from this wordplay because I knew it was how I would share "pieces of myself" with enough efficacy as an organic iced green tea infused with raspberry flavor to tell you, "Hey, it's me." My musings are like my tea: often deep but not steeped too early or too long. No matter how you digest the ponderings in this book and how you prepare your tea, I hope it's the perfect pairing to solve one existential crisis at a time. "MUSEcasting" starts with a simple thought that is shared publicly, through our circle of confidantes. It could also be a social media post that finds life and meaning when it reaches another heart, or it touches another soul longing to take refuge in words that cast comfort. When your intent is such, never drown them deep in the abyss of what's forgotten, or worse, compartmentalize them in that corner of your brain, branded as "ignored." I decided to put them out there with hopes of changing perspectives for the better — a goal that will probably need time, just like how steeping tea is the art of waiting for hot water to become magical.

I read somewhere that "it takes around 2000 tiny leaves to make one pound of finished tea." Drinking tea is the type of indulgence that is never rushed because there is enjoyment when it is savored by both aroma and flavor. Please digest the contents of this book the same way, unhurried. As you find yourself immersed in its pages, one musing after the other, notice that ideas flow in a rather more fluid way. I didn't want chapters to define themes because that's also how our thoughts flow: agile, spontaneous, and hence borderless. A page with a title means it's in storytelling mode, while those without it form part of my random "DND broody moments" switched on by my own experiences or taken away from conversations with friends (even strangers). I have conveniently added some anecdotes at the bottom of select pages to let readers have context around thoughts that I perhaps wrote during a phase of my life that I outgrew, or outlearned.

In the course of your reading, this book also creates special rendezvous points with nine question-and-tea pairings for your own contemplation. While coffee is officially "on vacation," I hope these pages provide an exciting respite for your appreciation of tea in general, alongside a question that will reify a typical tea session to a moment in your timeline that's rather hard to forget.

May you find solace in some of the pages that deal with prejudice; comfort in your journey of being found or finding a partner for your own "'til death do us part" story; conviction in fighting for your dreams or reinforcing the will to live in case you're battling a life-threatening disease. Even if you're on a page that you can't simply relate to, at least be open to the message it presents and simulate people in your life who may be identifying with the perspective framed by every page. If at least it fires up your empathy for others, then these words will find their home — perhaps with two cups of tea meeting from corner to center, as two individual experiences overlap with a sense of self-awareness, or even in the pursuit of understanding others.

We are here, both the musecaster in me and this book, to stir thoughts that may have been orphaned in the depths of your past, or as fresh as the tea bag that you just left in your cup to steep, but never with the intent, even remotely, of spilling the tea, literally and figuratively.

We don't need that kind of stain in our minds, or even on those immaculate white pants.

A new year clutches with it a hybrid of emotions.
Nonetheless, it is my most liberating time of the year.

As the hours dwindle towards a full transition from the current year to the next, it gives you a vivid flashback of how the year has gone by; memories of your struggles; fighting a disease; recovering from a calamity that you thought would have ended your life; making amends with a boss or colleague you had a hard time working with; finding a new love; meeting a stranger who probably took your breath away; dragging your feet to the lecture session you hated most.

It was all a journey that flew by in a year's time.

What you thought would never end or what you wished didn't end is finally going to go along with the last 24 hours of the year. In that last hour, you will ask yourself how you want those stories to end. Quell your worries and believe there is a wonderful ending that awaits, sometime between now and then.

Love without regret. What you felt at a specific time in your life, if you loved unconditionally, that is what's TRUE. You don't regret someone who made you happy. Loving is a choice and YOU made that choice. Don't wallow in regret, but LEARN.

Choose with discernment. Don't let bad choices change you. Instead, change your choice. We always want things our way but reality will find its timing to humble us and put us back to our places.

Be happy and be shameless about it. Do not look for a backroom door for guilt. Happiness has no extra room for that inconvenient guest. Happiness comes to those who appreciate it. Arrest it!

The best thing about New Year's Eve is how, for one night, you are able to feel how much you can love, live, and learn in between. It's a chance that we all receive.

Another shot. A new beginning.
Turn your life into a show no one dares to forget.

Everybody lies, albeit moot.
Not everyone can handle the truth either.

Life is too monumental to capture in social media. I see them as thumbnails, snippets of what happens out there, at times overly shared to make others smile or maybe empathize momentarily until they are marshaled by our own emotions. Then, there are some precious moments cherished privately. They're so good that you just want to steep in them, selfishly so.

Remember, we all have a choice about what others know about us, but the moment we put something out there, it becomes public. That becomes a target for people to praise, ridicule, or comment on. It takes a whole lot of mental preparation to be "unbothered" by such.

Don't let social media be "windows" that ruin the integrity of your life's events. You decide which ones to open or which ones to keep shut.

The past will never linger longer than you allow it to. The present will not be exciting until it's out of the past's shadows. The future is the best break you could ever give yourself. Through a string of transitional changes, we remember those people who are instrumental in safeguarding us to better days.

Through it all, only a grateful heart endures the battles. We don't merit more blessings on a whim or by making false claims. When you're soaked in gratitude, every experience becomes an opportunity to learn, or a chance to make amends. It loses sincerity when it is wrapped in so much drama.

Even in pain, we write our own stories in a way that makes us forgive ourselves and forget whatever (or whoever) left us with a hole. A grateful heart will endure days or years with missing pieces, only to fully appreciate the very reason when someday, it becomes whole once more.

One day, it will all make sense.
For now, heal anyway.

Be kind.
You don't need to have a reason to be so.
Be understanding.
You don't have to be understood to know how.
Be fair.
Our assumptions of others may not be true.
Be considerate.
Put "How others will feel" first before you make "What you say or do" a priority.
Be faithful.
This is not open for negotiation.
Be honest.
No one deserves to be fooled.
Be yourself.
The world deserves nothing more than your one true self.

We should find our own individual recipes for happiness. A slice of sincerity and a pinch of good judgment should be good for starters. Take a cupful of honesty because every person deserves that. Take generous servings of authenticity to infuse well with flavors. Serve with hefty portions of love.

If it boils too fast, give it time to calm down to a simmer. Happiness should not be rushed. Garnish with kindness because it's highly unlikely for people to reject it. Plate with a prayer that your happiness doesn't deprive others of theirs.

Sure, this recipe might be too flavorful to the taste of others, but remember this: their preferences should have no space in your own happiness.

Truth be told, there are some of us who love independence, but a few will oppose the "sweetness of wanting to be found."

Looking back at old photos, I can't help but surrender to the callings of my fervor for traveling. Just romancing with the idea of setting foot on a new destination consumes my whole being.

They say we have not lived if we have not traveled. We meet new friends, salivate over local cuisine, marinate in culture, and experience the world in a language that only a city can translate with so much of its character.

There's anxiety over what awaits us, only to be overwhelmed by the revelation of lives, especially those different from ours. It is always humbling. While we lose ourselves in the experience, we realize deep down who we are and how far or close we are from who we want to be.

Every parent wishes to be perfect.
Every child wishes their parents have standards that are anything *but* perfect.

Appreciation is a constant, not a variable. It shouldn't also be selective.

We remember people for the good that they've done. While we immerse ourselves in the thought that "we are worth it," we should also make them feel that they have that room carved in our lives. Every person we are grateful for fits into that space we shaped for them perfectly.

There's absolutely nothing wrong with wishing for something out of this world. That's why dreams exist. What's more important is that when you snap out of those moments, they leave your heart in its happy beat with the thought of clean clothes, a warm bed, food on the table, and people who love you for just the way you are. It takes grace to appreciate what you have. If we can't enjoy what's in front of us, we are not prepared for bigger things to come.

(To those with partners) It's so sweet to wake up to the thought that
we belong to someone.
(To those longing) It's so exciting to know who that someone will
be.
Positivity is always a matter of perspective.

Healing

Like Masala tea, which is best served with just the right amount of milk to your preference, this question should be asked with caution.

Who made the deepest cut in your heart and who stitched it up to be whole again?

The things you take for granted, someone else is praying for. Another girl wishes to experience trips that you think are a waste of time.

We think that the same route we take going to work is unremarkable, while a little boy just yearns that he would be able to walk again.

A man wonders about his next big purchase to show that he made it in life, while a homeless grandfather waits for the next penny to fall into his hat on the floor.

We complain about waiting for our turn in a restaurant queue while someone mentally thanks the exact moment that he gets to wait; that he has time while some others are deprived of it.

The ironies in this world are so extreme that sometimes it takes stripping away entitlement to give more meaning to what we see as ordinary.

It takes humility to understand that waking up to another day is a privilege.

A power thought to single ladies out there:
Go for the man who will always choose *you*, even when other options are accessible.

No one expects you to be perfect.
Sometimes we succeed
Some other times we don't.
Be comfortable with just the idea of being your best self.
When you find that place, no criticism or compliment can ever
distract you.

There are people who put in so much effort posting about what "consumes" them, briefly or permanently. Whether it's food that they are about to eat, the inch-detailing of growing babies, or even cryptic musings that tide people over to their big reveal, don't relegate them to being "trivial."

People often forget that these are all part of someone's life shared with readers. If we don't pay attention, the loss is ours. If we don't intend to be "sociable" that way, let alone care enough to understand their social media preoccupation of the moment, this isn't the right space and place for us.

Self-expression comes in various shapes, tones, and forms. How others do theirs does not necessarily have to conform to ours, and vice versa.

The happiest people on earth are not those who have everything they need. They're the ones who give even with the little they have. Sometimes that means giving up their own share.

Happiness is not about finding reasons why we should be happy. Nothing in its true existence is about "us."

Look at how the "I" has perfect placement in the word "happiness." In any direction, there are other letters that would have to come first; others first.

Look for reasons why today you have to put someone else's care before yours; give up something for someone. Wake up to that same thought and see how that changes your perspective from superficial to phenomenal!

Say this to someone today,
"I love you with the kind of love more than my heart can hold."

You, yes you.

You may have been a "serial" liker or one of those I unintentionally drowned in my feed. Frankly, my dear, I notice.

There were years in our lives that have proven to be a storming wind of change, in a good way. For me, 2014 was indeed a time of "waking up" to live a dream. Not that life has always been a walk in the park. It's just that as we get older, we learn better to appreciate who and what we have and flee from what we ordinarily want. Through it all, wise people have taken it to heart to battle changes with acceptance – which is good.

I remember saying, "I'd get married at 28." I fooled myself with my own expectations. However, I learned that single people appreciate the feeling of "freedom"; to do as they please and go to places without guilt or the need for permission. We continue to admire those with families and respect them for how they make ends meet and how they traded a life of single-and-swinging to a lifetime commitment of thinking for any number more than one. The truth of the matter is there is no perfect status. There are married people who are miserable; there are single folks who are desperate. Don't let status define our level of happiness.

It is so tempting to judge people on the surface. Stop. Right. There. We have no idea what they are going through. Worse, for any of us to think and assume their post is about us is really just kind of overrated. The sun revolves around the earth, not just you. Like the narrative if it makes you smile, scroll down if it means nothing to you. Don't judge. Don't mock. Or just don't be on social media. If you've decided to befriend the person and unless you're the patronizing type, that decision was yours, not theirs.

Then there's the other side of the fence. When we're the ones putting ourselves out there: perhaps you got married, or had a baby, traveled to Reykjavík, and have been dying to share online, no one can stop you from doing that. Be prepared, though, that once it goes "public" it will draw attention and reaction from others, and the moment you let them affect you, it defeats the whole purpose of sharing. If you see a comment that is not true, believe me when I say that "it's not worth your time."

As long as your post resonates with one reader, there is a good purpose for your post. If it helped you ease your trouble by socializing it, that's one step closer to self-awareness. That's a sure win that nobody else can discount.

Be angry. Be giddy. Thank your village and tag their names if it makes you happy. Be jealous. Be affected. That's being human. Don't forget to move on. Don't get stuck with an emotion when the rest of the world has forgotten. There is a plethora of social media traps everywhere. Remember, you control what goes on "out there" and not the other way around.

Be fearless. Untangle yourself from your comfort zone. Be kind, especially to someone who cannot do anything for you. Be beautiful, talented, and smart. Gone are the days when people who are attractive are "supposed" to be dumb. Yes, you read that right. Now move along. Be happy. You owe this to yourself. This one is solely on you. Find a new hobby. Read more books. Visit a chapel for no reason. Greet a nasty stranger. Send a note to yourself. Fall. In. Love. Kiss someone who believes you're worth it. Choose a healthier lifestyle. Gain friends. Drink wine. Ditch the beer. Show up to an all-black event wearing marsala red. Do something that scares you. Everyday. Travel to a place you've never been. Take someone who enjoys long walks. Learn a new language. Have constant dates with your parents. Spend what you saved. Be responsible with how you do that. Volunteer. Make every "now" count. Laugh like a hyena. Look at the sky when you walk outdoors. Don't trip. Don't mess with other people's hearts. Go to a city with a name you can't even pronounce.

Do everything that keeps you real.

Next to Board and Never Bored

An American businessman was seated at the exit row behind me. He was casually conversing with a Filipino guy (who we'll call Mr. Kind Man) who was nice enough to "engage" in a verbal exchange. With our flight delayed by a few minutes, I was asked to make a halt right before the aircraft door at hearing distance from them. Mr. Kind Man was trying to call the ground staff but to no avail. After his fourth attempt, I decided to use my trusty vocal power to get the staff's attention. Mr. Kind Man asked for the staff to expedite the bus because there was a passenger with an onward flight to General Santos boarding at 0620H: time check, 0635H. The staff looked puzzled, but she said a bus was on its way. Putting all the pieces together "Little Miss Philippines" (me) had to join the "assisting party." I explained the situation to the staff in these exact words: "Hi, you are with ground passenger handling, right? Can you radio the Philippine Airlines flight (he's coming from a carrier different from PR, obviously) to General Santos to confirm that one of their passengers is here and will take that flight? She then asked for the last name. I looked at the American, expecting that I would surprise him, being a new "character" in his story, but he gracefully responded with his last name. Most of the time, I have a hard time hearing so I said, "Can I see your boarding pass please?" I then relayed the exact flight number with his last name to the staff and gave him back his pass. He smiled and thanked me in return.

A bus came in less than 10 seconds later. On board the bus, Mr. Kind Man explained that he was trying to help the American businessman and he extended his gratitude to me. I said he did the right thing and it had a domino effect on me. By the end of this short ride, we were recipients of multiple thank yous and smiles from fellow passengers.

If we care enough, we have to do more than just "watch." We can't change the world instantly but we can help make it better, even if it's for one stranger at a time.

When you freely allow people to express themselves (without fear of reprimand), or make mistakes (with promise to help them rise when they fall), they grow.
They learn to be comfortable in their own skin.
They respect differences.
They engage in good conversations without assuming it will turn into a debate.
They learn to coexist with others without the need to validate their superiority.
They don't need to mask their insecurities.
They learn to value creating an identity that is uniquely theirs, not a mold of someone that they have to fit into.

Love will not always come in a shape and form known to us. It is not convenient all the time. It is not always what we perceive as gentle and "wise." What we say about other people is not about them. It's about us. Let's not make fools of ourselves by saying we do things for love unless it really is about "less of yourself and more of others."

It will hurt. It will sting. It will not patronize and make you the "king." Sometimes, it's the only brave feeling that fills that empty space between people. It will not hide or disguise an agenda. Or hide under the blankets of friendship.

In rare cases, after all that's told and unspoken, it finally finds its nest in acceptance. We don't necessarily end up with the "man of the moment" or the "woman of our wishes." People do not always walk away because they stop loving.

Sometimes, for the better, they finally know what they deserve.

People are always waiting.
For that "big break,"
For someone;
For another chance;
For cure;
For an end to something;
Or a new beginning.
There is always that pause.
We deal with that differently. We wonder. We ask questions. We waste chances. We stay. We leave. We walk away. They say good things happen to those who wait. Others say, life happens when we stop waiting. Different strokes for different folks. We believe what helps us cope with this long wait.
No matter where we are in this journey, trust that not too far along is a full stop, a curve, or a waiting shed. Take time to pray, think, and exhale.
Trust that you are where you are meant to be.
Because the last one wasn't your bus;
Because there's a free seat in the next one just for you — and it's coming.

Mindfulness

Black tea comes from fermented leaves and tastes stronger than others due to caffeine. This next question solicits awareness and is best paired with tea that compliments it with improved focus and alertness.

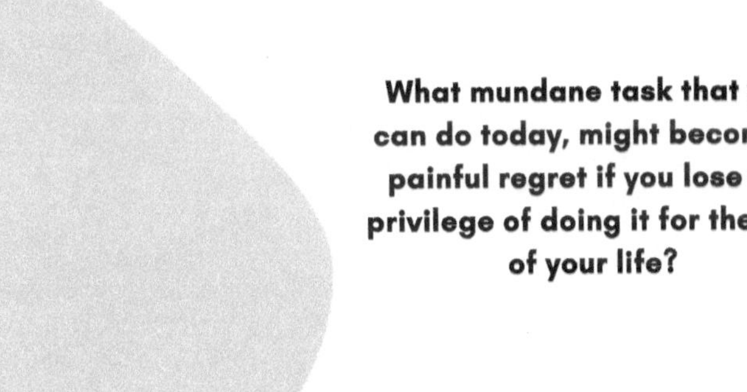

What mundane task that you can do today, might become a painful regret if you lose the privilege of doing it for the rest of your life?

Somewhere along the lines of forever, between what I want and what He planned, are those stories we chose to write ourselves. Admit it: they're not the best stories ever told. They remind us, though, that we've lived. There is always another door other than the one that closed. Always.

At some point, we will all have to let go. The wheel keeps on turning, but we can only see as far as the bumper lights go. Let go so He can take control. His hand will not make a mistake, but it will teach lessons. When faith is like shifting sands, you just have to surrender and let the waters take you to shore.
Almost there.
Almost learned.
Always saved by faith.

I don't know where I am going. I just know I am leaving this place: this home of "comfort." It's a cry for change. Baffling as how some may look at it, I am always the "girl who knows what she wants." Recently, tides have seemingly gone a different direction. Like everything else, this, too, will pass. I don't know how or when, but I know he will find me. Out there awaits an intersection where my dreams and fate meet. I have been through some hurdles recently, and the humps may have slowed me down, but even collectively, they have not shifted those hopes, unwavering. "Where reason ends, faith begins." I wrote that in an old blog ten thousand flips of pages back, but I heard someone say it recently. I wonder how people find that "common place" despite our differences, like even with a multitude of thoughts, we stumble upon someone who probably went through a similar trail and ended up touching the same stone. So, it's there: away from public radar, between my mind and my heart, I protect that lingering flame of hope, of love, of forever. They say people change their minds and hearts. I have always challenged that until today when I am confronted by apathy for overfamiliarity. I just told a friend recently that I want to be far, far, far away from here. I had to say it repetitively in the hopes that this universe would hear my small voice and succumb to the wishes of a spirit wanting to be free. Chained by expectations, my core is screaming for change. It's so loud that I know it's bound to be heard somehow. So far, I have been getting the same response, echoing through the confined walls of "patience hall." Not. Just. Yet. I know in my heart I have given so much and I'm not expecting anything back. That's love in my world — 'til it hurts. Until it hurts. Someone out there deserves it.

Good vibes don't always come in the brightest color and in the loudest parade. Sometimes, it is ushered by the sheer honesty of silence.

I know deep down the universe listens.
And there's that spot. Somewhere in the plush corner of your heart, nests a dream that's potent enough to survive. Even the most heartbreaking truth failed to break down its barriers because it has kept hope intact. It's a place where we remain unscathed. They say

that nothing and no one hurts over the idea of something "that has not happened yet."

That empty chair. It's been open for as long as I can remember. Somehow, in the whole waiting game, I have "temporarily assigned" that space to someone that I perhaps liked momentarily. No one has taken permanent ownership of that "plus one" title. Not just yet. He's still out there. So, the chair stays here.

I am one to overly share thoughts and emotions because, in one way or another, they help others take on that personal jaunt within. What's been put out there for public consumption is far from the "whole story." There's a lot about this life that we write about. There's a lot more about me that I choose to keep within the confines of privacy. They, too, take residence in that corner of my heart that I keep alive. It's a collection of "what I want to feel," a reminder of what I choose to marinate in, of what is privately mine and mine alone. It's a place where I am less vulnerable because I protect my heart, and rightfully so.

It's been a while, and I have not entirely let anyone in. They say it's worth taking risks for. I get that. In the end though, I am personally responsible for my heart — which is the only one that I have. It would not hurt to be a little more sure and a little more cautious the next time I choose to give it away — or so I feel. The man without a name is yet to be found. My hand will not touch another's because it's rightfully waiting for his. At least that part of my dream stays lucid.

Anecdote: I wrote this piece while living my status as a perennially single woman with "yearning" so loud you can feel it in every word. If you are in a similar state, please believe that the chair is empty because there's a rightful person for that space and either that person is out there living events that lead to you, or that chair is meant for you when you would choose to sit on it happily. My husband eventually found that chair, and now we've put our chairs next to each other in direct view of sunrises and sunsets.

They say that love is blind. I say it is a decision. It appears blinding to people who do not understand why you made that choice, yet your decision holds. Love is not just seeing the "agreeable" aspects of someone's personality. It's the acceptance that there is a side of them that could potentially hurt us, yet we love just the same.

They say "love means not having to say you're sorry." Regret, for me, is healthy to a point when you realize that you've made a mistake. Admission humbles everyone and prepares us to learn to love again, even better the next time around. The overall experience is nothing to regret, especially if it leaves us with lessons.

Love is limitless. It is neither constrained by social status nor by the resources that we have. The more of it we share, the more selfless we become. Love is forgiving. It doesn't wait for a reason to give chances. If we don't know how to forgive, remember how we were forgiven. It doesn't require an apology (something that I recently learned). It is the golden secret to having peace of mind. It silences all doubts.

Love is grateful. It exalts in every act or word of kindness that is unselfishly wrapped in sincerity. It appreciates the giver for the gesture, over and above what is materially given. It acts as the "white picket fence" to a happy heart. (I love that image!)

Love is transcending. It overcomes pride, prejudice, and judgment. It is not selective that way. What harm can it do if we just love anyway? It's the whole point of our existence.

Love is unconditional. It is not mindful of how much it has received because the desire to give more wins by comparison.

Love is not a secret. It is not meant to be hidden in the dark corners of shame or betrayal. It is given away freely, with the object of our affection fully knowing why we are here. If it's hidden, you should not be in it.

Love is not processed. Unlike thoughts, it rests in the heart, where everything good is nurtured and nursed. Logic is far too complicated to handle.

To all my married friends, remember the day you made that vow. No matter how long you've been struggling in your marriage, it doesn't change why you chose to be together. If I had the power, I'd protect that and hope you realize how much you have been blessed with — a partner. Love is a commitment.

To all my single friends: the search is far from over. Waiting is meant to grow that love outside boundaries you thought you could never break. Somewhere out there, he is wishing for you. Love is hope.

There is no greater gift than LOVE. If you lose it, find it again. If you break it, heal and then be brave again. Don't stop until you get the happy ending you deserve.

Love resides in good. If you're sharing love, you're making this world much better than it was yesterday.

Love is happiness. It makes you smile even in silence, knowing you are in a much better place now.

Of the many lessons I have learned, I keep one closest to my heart — "Loving more" is a lifetime purpose.

What if I did something in the past that altered my own course? What if I said something differently that brought me here, instead of "there," that somehow got me a different set of friends? What if we haven't met?

Ask me today, and I wouldn't change a thing. For someone who takes things at face value (and rocks her brain analyzing them a few seconds later), I don't like living in "what ifs."

No one gets married thinking it will fall apart. No one gets into a friendship thinking that the same person will talk about you behind your back. Yes, we have our expectations and when things do not go as planned, that's when we get hurt. This is the exact point when we wonder over "what ifs" and torture ourselves trying to trace our steps back, asking, "What did I do wrong, or at which point did I make a mistake?"

Stop. Don't.

Truth be told, no one has the answer. You just have to believe that things didn't happen the way you planned them to be but they are in His hands. We are too stubborn to get something better, but He's preparing the BEST.

Eat. Go for nutrient-dense food choices.

Exercise. It can change your appearance without going under the knife and change your outlook without seeing an expensive shrink.

Be grateful. It multiplies blessings exponentially.

Apologize. Humility can never harm your disposition in life.

Forgive. It's not difficult if you try… again then again.

Take a vacation. We have not lived until we have seen how others did. Sometimes, we just need some bit of "time off."

I'm a writer. Or so I feel. I take refuge in words and spaces because life is worth writing about. When I write, I live twice. There are no "what ifs" if we have faith.

No matter what path we choose, it always ends up in one destined point — where he is standing, waiting to hold my hand.

Life just is.

To me, it's a love story that is well-written. He's still out there. What do you say to someone who will start your "forever?" — "I will see you soon."

Anecdote: This was clearly during a time when being single made me found another "fingers-on-keyboard" moment.

Happiness is an "inside job." Never give the control to someone else's hands. Laugh. It keeps the soul young. Love. It keeps you inspired. Forgive even when it hurts. Be somebody to someone. Cry. Give your sorrows an exit door they deserve. Travel. The world awaits. Live well. You owe it to yourself. You see, you don't need a reason to be happy. Be here, in the moment, and embrace the surprise, whatever it may be. Life will not always go as planned and that's okay.

Be happy and be very good at it.

Before we speak of kindness, think of people we've hurt along the way.
Before we preach about being right, remember the last person we wronged and have not apologized to.
Before we brag about raising kids well, prepare to give runway to understanding how they feel.
Before saying we always win, think of the last person we lost because they decided to leave.

I hope you fall in love with someone who tells you he misses you when you're rows apart in the same aircraft; or someone who holds your hand when you walk in the park. I hope you fall in love with someone who says, "No worries, I'll get it," when you forget to do an errand that was supposedly for him; someone who never forgets that you still like getting handwritten letters. I hope you fall in love with someone who sends you a random text to show that you're remembered; someone who'll never walk ahead or behind you. I hope you fall in love with someone who shamelessly kisses you in the rain. I hope you fall in love with someone who calls you "mine" like it's your first name.

I hope you fall in love with someone who doesn't necessarily make you his whole life — but the part he can't live without.

Between the depth of the waters and the vastness of blue skies, you have to find that space you can call yours. Find friends who are true enough to laugh and cry with you until that void becomes whole again. Take yourself lightly and treat mistakes as a reminder of the imperfection that will keep you grounded. Others will say things about you and they're entitled to their opinion. Truth resides in a heart of solid faith. Not all battles are worth putting out a fighting stance for. Fall in love with life. Fall out of bad relationships. Rise to every occasion where you can show to the world who you are, stripped of any form of pretension, insecurity, and envy. You are made different because you *are* different. Never, not even for one faulty instance, think that you are better or worse than others. The only comparison we should make is what the heart beats for versus what the mind wills to achieve. Somewhere in between, that's where you find your *one true self.*

Someday, someone will find himself special enough to deserve you.

If you have a shot at "forever," why would you settle for "in the meantime?"

Apologies are meant to be given, not explained. They are not conditional on what the other party should do or accept before they are given.

Apologizing doesn't require turning tables to blame someone else for his/her wrongdoing, or defend an intention.

The outcome is not what either one or both of the parties expected.
Recognize the results for what they are.
Apologize.
Move on and do better.

"I am sorry" is a full sentence that can stand on its own. It is not a sign of weakness or defeat. Being able to say it without "ifs" or "buts" is a show of strong willpower that yields to humility — and that takes fortitude. Collectively, that builds character.

Peace of Mind

Milder than the black tea, Oolong tea ranges from "light to full bodied, floral to grassy, and sweet to toasty," and is often associated with side effects of weight loss. Living life to the fullest also means offloading the "unpleasantries." This question hopefully precipitates leaving some of that unnecessary weight behind.

How do you deal with the worst thing that someone has said about you?

Frustrations will wear us down before we get it right but if we don't spend this life loving, we're not living.
Sometimes a void frees up so something new can take its place.
For the best
For happier endings
Forgiven

The liberating thing about being 40 is I no longer aim to please the crowd around me. I can step out of the house, or sashay down the streets of another country, minding only what I choose to comfortably wear.
I am not an object of everyone's judgment.
Whatever they say is an opinion.
I remain to be the fact.

The nice thing about being who I am is that I can wake up every morning armed with equable faith, rather than uncertainty. Worrying is pointless because what's bound to happen, will happen and ultimately, it's about learning to forgive others and myself.

It's liberating to know that I don't need validation from anyone. Compliment is inspiring and criticism is brutal. I don't let the former get to my head. I don't let the latter mess with my heart. Point is, to not let them change who I have aspired to become.

The cool thing about being 40 is that I don't require social acceptance. The only approval I need for decisions that range from sartorial to professional is mine. It's juvenile to blame someone; mercurial to follow the trend and frustrating to even need approval from others.

Whoever I have in my life right now — those who chose to stick with me even in the thick of things — are the only ones who really matter. Out of seven billion people in the world today, I am blessed to have a squad, a tribe, a family that I can call mine. The entire universe doesn't have to know. Most of the time, all I need is one.

The interesting thing about being me, is I don't have to conform to a design. I become my own signature. Authenticity is my brand. Positive influence is my purpose. Where matters of intention are concerned, I don't owe the world any explanation.

Where the comfort and convenience of the shores are unquestionably inviting, turning another year older is always a riptide of change. While most will fear the abyss of what's unfamiliar, I'd rather swim with the current.

It's the age when an old paradigm takes a very brave shift: To tell myself that evolving to this new character defined by age is not being rude — it's keeping things honest.

Anecdote: I wrote this when I turned 40 but you get to decide your own time, and when you're ready to brave similar changes.

Curiosity that Cares

Some years ago, my parents shared this wonderful story.

Mom had to go to the drugstore to deal with her nagging leg pain and while waiting for her turn at the counter, an old man, who had a persistent shaking hand, caught her attention. Since curiosity runs insatiably in the family, she asked my dad to check on the man and ask what was keeping him waiting, oddly distant from the counter. The old man quipped that he needed to buy medicine for epileptic attacks, but he was short by a few pesos. Dad asked how much he needed. My folks handed a little over than the amount he needed and saw him approach the counter to get his prescription drugs. Before getting out of the drugstore, Mom handed him another bill and said, "Please get yourself a decent meal. You might need to eat before you take your meds."

The old man then left after he thanked my parents.

Don't do anything only to please others.
Drink water like it's the only thing that will keep you alive.
Choose the high road.
Pick your battles.
Apologize even if your mistake was unintentional.
Make amends.
Say hello to a friend you haven't talked to in years.
Smile at a stranger.
Help someone you don't know.
Give, even when you don't have enough.

The best feelings in the world need no explanation.
They just need to be chosen.

She always wants to be somewhere else. It shows in the way she's always rushing, moving; the way she's always restless. Her heart is always between two places. There's no point in asking her, or that heart, to be still.

You don't say goodbye to a place that you've been to. You don't return unchanged. It's like melody meeting harmony and when one tries to separate them, the music is never going to be the same. Those memories provide the rhythm. Don't ever make the mistake of thinking that when we travel, nothing changes. Your perception changes. That's practically everything.

Drive change. Embrace change. Be the change.

Take risks. Calculated ones are safest in comfort zones but those beyond our humanly possible imagination are worth stories of a lifetime. You have a choice between telling the story, listening to it, or having the story be about you. Decide for yourself.

Betrayal. Lack of gratitude. Arrogance. These three will not bring you success or peace of mind. There is always a higher road. Don't just walk to reach it. Run.

Don't ever go to sleep without remembering who you helped or hurt and find your own resolve. Never wake up ungrateful. Whatever happens, don't ever forget who helped you along the way. If you have to choose between these last three reminders, take the last one to heart.

Intelligence is a gift. Relationships take time and effort to build. Goodwill is a choice. Experience is the true test of our threshold for each one of them is a measure of who we've become.

If today is the last day we have to live, what will people say about you?
If tomorrow is the only time we have left, what would you do today?
If yesterday had a chance for a do-over, what would you do differently?

Time is never in our hands.
Go out. Live. Love. Learn.
Make the most out of what we have left.

Maturity is measured by knowing the right thing to say even when it's the most inconvenient time, choosing to walk away from an egotistical battle, and keeping silent to reaffirm that we are in a much better place.

Education helps us learn. Experience leaves us with wisdom. Maturity is a personal journey. You know you've arrived when you care enough to recognize others' struggles, and you remember how you got there in the first place. We don't judge. We don't mock. We don't parade. We sing and dance even without a marching band. We are happy with who we are, even when no one is watching.

Maturity doesn't compel us to prove anything. The fact that we are here, that we survived the past, is a statement in itself. We stop comparing ourselves with others. The only standard that exists is goodwill; what we have done to others, not what they think of us.

We don't feel the need to explain if only to have the last laugh. The only voice we hear is that which goes by the name "conscience." No fad changes our character. No compliment bloats our heads. No criticism makes those knees soft. We remember who we are, where we came from, and who helped us to get even a little farther than wherever that was.

We forgive.
We accept defeat.
We move on with grace and humility; never with arrogance.
We don't complain.
In some lonely corner of this universe, someone is living a life harder than ours. No amount of eloquence, passport stamps, or bank accounts can change who we are. If we don't love that version of ourselves, it would be unfair to expect more from this world. When you've found the map that shows the quickest way to get there, please show the rest of us how. Meanwhile, it's still a labyrinth, and we're all on the same ground, looking for that place where silence is, at times, the most effective way to communicate.
Not a preacher — just a girl here who lives to try for a change; for the better. They say we should count our blessings. Every year on the day I was born (honor and thanks to the most selfless parents I

know), I take time to read (and reply to) every message sent my way. Nothing gets more personal than that. For the inveterate writer that I am, every note brings back special moments turned into memories with you all. Whether those took five minutes or five years, you and I share a story that we laughed at, cried about, or learned from. When you remember someone on her special day, imagine a wellspring of emotions opening up and flooding disposition with so much positivity. It's a lucid reminder of how I became this person that I didn't even imagine becoming; of how I got here from the humble comforts of my childhood.

Mom etched a very good lesson in my head when I was much younger that it found residence in my heart: "What you don't have, you don't need." It's a life meant to be lived in contentment. We do have dreams, and we will continue to aspire for something "more." While that is good and bold, nothing beats genuine peace of mind from knowing what we have is enough and believing that there will always be enough to share with others. It's not what others did or said in the past that keeps every story alive. It's how they continue to remember that I am part of their lives and they are part of mine.

I am one to saturate thoughts and musings without intent to preach, but with hopes that readers will have some takeaways from "what I learned."

Do something every day that matters to someone else. Say something to yourself that you wouldn't want to hear from somebody, not even your best friend. Take in the most cut-throat criticism you've received and listen without challenging it. Let that put you back to your place. Forgive someone who left you at your worst. Forget every pain by praying gratefully for someone who keeps you at your best. Honor mom and dad. Do the very thing that scares you. Travel to a place you've been eyeing on Instagram or a place you've been itching to see again. Drink lots of water. Apologize. It doesn't make you less of a person to do so. It cures — the other person's wounds and yours. Whoever said something bad about you is basking in guilt. The only vengeance I know is to live happily. If others don't care, show them how to do it. The world

may or may not thank you for it, but you'll feel good about it — and
that is priceless.

This is my life, yet it is His story.
Thank you for continuing to flip pages.

The most enduring friendships are like the great vast sky. They change with seasons and reasons, but you know that they are there. Even the most memorable moments have to set like the sun, taciturn as they seem, distanced by time. Count on it though that they will rise and surface again like the sunrise, without fail. There is no room for jealousy or competition. Such friendships do not use "better or worse" as a metric. In the same way, neither bright stars nor the blinding rays of the sun intimidate the sky. It's bigger than all those parts combined. It has that kind of love big enough to allow everyone to do what they are meant to do — and shine.

"The distance between pain and healing is as short as the space between your knees and the floor."

Someone told me this at a point in my life when my heart was so broken. I mentally returned to these words as soon as I reached my heartbreak sobriety and realized it was the exact line that left me — unbroken.

Anecdote: Someone said these words to me when I was delusionally broken-hearted. I hope they find their way to nurse yours.

We are not complete. We are works in progress. Gone are those days when we can be easily fooled by those who just patronize. We are human beings, not objects of one's opinion or desire. Between successes and failures, choose to learn. Love to move on. We are far from perfect, but be strong enough to face what comes our way. We are in love, by our definition of it, with life and those we choose to keep for our lifetime. Good is everywhere around us. Be a voyager in that sense. Learn to be a traveler, not just a tourist. The world awaits those with insatiable curiosity for what's not within our comfort zone. Be a storyteller because life is too short for experiences not to be spoken about. We like a lot of people in this world, and we love maybe a few.

Don't be a proponent of negativity, whichever form it comes. It ages us, and I haven't found the elixir of youth more powerful than being "just happy." If it's bad, nip it in the bud. If it's good, spread it like an epidemic. When we talk about others, we reveal ourselves. When we talk about ourselves, we are deprived of the gift of others. No one wants to be limited by what people think of us. Go your own way and live your story. What other people say is either a compliment or a criticism, and both are founded on opinion. Never mistake any of these two as a definition of you.

We are flawed. We are imperfect. As long as we remain honest with those around us, without any intention to hurt or cause pain, there will be no sleepless nights. A battle is always between good and bad. Choose good without fail or doubt.

If we have to fight, make sure it's for the benefit of someone or something else. Otherwise, walk away. We can't always win by engaging. We cannot change the world, but we can change ourselves.

This world doesn't deserve to give residence to people who don't care. Prove that we are worth its air and resources. Take care of it and it will reveal how magnificent every space is between sky and soil.

When we look away, we see the promise of hope. When we look up, we see the revelation of His plans. When we look down, we feel humbled by our feet kissing the ground. When we look at each other, we feel a powerful connection. Put down those gadgets and learn to communicate again.

There is no age at which we should start working towards becoming awesome and amazing, so I say it's any time, when we're ready to begin.

Purpose

We all want to start and end our days free from stress and headaches. Peppermint tea is the perfect choice to usher your thoughts to tackle this next question, as its refreshing flavor will enhance cognition.

Who or what do you wake up for every morning?

We should all choose to live a life that's happy. We evangelize good. We disentangle ourselves from any form of negativity. Don't be limited by others and their expectations of you. The only limitation we have resides in self-doubt and fear. Don't let anyone sponsor those contraries.

Even if we only know how to do one thing, be very good at it. Turn it into personal branding and bother less about being perfect for the world. Those who are worth keeping will always appreciate you, no matter what.

After I was briefly silenced in admiration by one of Balkan's gems, North Macedonia's Lake Ohrid, I turned around for a photo, and the next moment turned out to be the best story I ever told.

With the famous Church of St. John at Kaneo atop the hill as a backdrop, his hand appeared clutching a small box and the rest was a "yes" going down officially to "our" history.

Where genuine displaces grandeur of words or action, the world suddenly came down to just him, me, and the moment that punctuated my could-have-and-might-have-been stories with a period.

This was when I realized that my favorite travel arrangement would then change from "just one" to a "plus one" and involve wiser decisions about the destination — "anywhere with him."

Anecdote: This page is lovingly dedicated to my husband, Alvin. He decided to pop the question during the first stop of our Balkan trip in 2018. I guess not all hearts are left in San Francisco.

"MINE."
It takes one word to turn someone into a shopaholic.

When Less is Definitely More

While traveling along SLEX, my husband craved "fried chicken," so we went to one of those big gas stations with fast food restaurants for late lunch.

Five spoons of rice later, our silence was broken by the sound of utensils clunking on the floor. We saw a dad carrying a half-emptied tray. He was bringing food back to his family when a kid rushed to the door to follow his mom and accidentally hit the tray from the dad's blind corner. The dad was stunned, not knowing whether to pick up the mess or call out the kid. For seconds, we saw the kid's mom outside, watching it all happen. After a few seconds more, the kid and mom walked away like nothing happened.

The dad brought food to their table, trying to explain to his wife and kid what had happened. He was at a loss as to what to do next. I knew the store would replace it (because the accident occurred within the store), and lo and behold, a food attendant brought them a fresh order of exactly what fell on the floor. The dad gushed and said "Thank you" in disbelief that the store made up for the accident.

People behind our tables expressed disgust over the kid's mom, who didn't even offer to pay or replace the spilled drink and food. Then I asked my husband, "What if the mom spent all her money for the weekend to bring her kids here; what if she got scared since she had no money left?" My husband said (and I totally agree), "Then at least muster some decency to say 'I'm sorry.'"

As my mind just conveniently decided to retire to people-watching, a couple behind my husband was feasting over a plate of chicken with gravy, when another female attendant brought large fries to their table. The couple didn't even look her way and continued munching. Bubble thoughts: "They didn't even say 'thank you?' I shared my observation with my husband again (by this time, I'm sure he's convinced he married a "nosy" woman). He shook his head and shrugged his shoulders. I said, "This is just too frustrating to watch."

Before we left the restaurant, the dad (yes, from the first scene) was ushering his son to the restroom when he came across one of the food attendants. He said, "Thank you again for your kindness, for replacing our food that fell on the floor." These words merited a smile from the food attendant, tailed by a proper "Welcome."

My husband missed that scene, so I recapped it for him. I said that a "*thank you*" came from the same man deprived of an "*I'm sorry.*"

No matter how each day gets rough and tough I go back to this confluence of ups and downs to remind myself of anything and everything good despite some bumps on the road. I don't pray for roses. I pray for resilience against thorns. I don't ask for easy. I pray for strength to overcome the difficulties. I don't desire for negativity to go away. I humbly ask for a shower of kindness. Even in the most awkward and inconvenient times, those boons never stop surfacing when they are "timely." It makes me wonder why we wait for Thanksgiving or Christmas to show appreciation for everything we should be grateful for.

It was another day worth celebrating that we are alive and safe. We got to live, love, and laugh for one more day. Tomorrow will present itself without guarantee of anything easier or happier. I just choose to say, "It's not going to get the best of me today."

Out of the ten things that could go wrong our way, choose one that makes everything feel right again.

May we have less of opinion and more of acceptance.
May we learn to forgive and need fewer reasons to be forgiven.
May we bridge, not break.
May we worry less.
May we age wisely.
May we love unconditionally.
May we live happily.
May we laugh incessantly.
Most of all, may we live that life that we always pray for.

If you are filled with hate, I hope you are soon overwhelmed by so much love around you.
If you are unwell, I wish you are restored to good health.
If you are in doubt, I pray that faith finds you.
If you are experiencing emotional, financial, or professional unrest, I hope you find serenity in prayer.
If you are searching for meaning, I hope you get fulfillment in giving.
If today isn't working for you, I hope tomorrow pleasantly surprises you.
If you are hurting, I pray that you heal.

I travel, therefore, I am.
I love, therefore, I exist.
I hurt, therefore, I am human.
I forgive, therefore, I welcome peace of mind.
I forget, therefore, I make mistakes.
I learn, therefore, I do better.

I write, therefore, I live twice.

Whatever caused your thoughts to be arrested;
Whoever crippled your imagination; however deflated your sense of
hope may be, just remember:

It only takes a brand new day to tell your worries, "Your time is up!
Today is mine, and I'm about to change my disposition for the
better."

Be old enough to know you live your life on your own terms.
Be strong enough to accept why we can't have or change everything.
Be wise enough to mind who matters and shield yourself from pensive thoughts.
Be kind enough to forgive even those who hurt you.
Be happy enough to stay unbothered by others' opinions.
Be brave enough to admit you are wrong, to clobber your judgment of others.
Be passionate enough to give your dream the oxygen it deserves.
Be sensitive enough to think everyone goes through something they want to speak or be silent about.
Be bold enough to just be your one authentic self.
We may not get credit for all of these, but purpose is precious.

Others' opinions and reactions should NOT change your intention.

I don't have everything.
I am far from perfect.
I don't own what others possess.
I don't have ties with anyone powerful in the government.
I don't know how to bake.
I am not affiliated with well-known last names in the country.
I don't have a title that people should envy.
I don't go home to a three-bedroom penthouse with an ocean view.

What society sometimes dictates as measures of success is irrelevant to how we define our standards.
I have our parents and family members in better health.
I have very smart niblings.
I have a husband who's loving and kind.

We have dogs who show us unconditional love and loyalty.
We have a small space we rightfully call our home.
We have roof above our heads, food on the table, clean drinking water every day.
We have jobs that give opportunities and recognition to what we do.

I have friends, old and new, who will swear by our friendships.
I have "sisters" who prove friendships can be thicker than blood.
I have today.
I have hope.
I have dreams.
I have this life.
They are ENOUGH.

May every new year unfold immeasurable kindness and the kind of healing that dulls every pain felt.

Love to the fullest, despite ourselves.

Second Chances

If there is a pseudo-name for the humble tea, Green tea would have my vote. Noted for its simplicity and relaxing effect, the benefits of this tea range from improving attention to being friendly to the gut. It has antioxidant properties. What more can we ask for? Well, an answer to this next question will top the cup.

What decision have you made in the past would you change today, assuming you have the opportunity to do so?

The best stories are never put on display. They're shared around a table with trusted friends, most loved family members, or whispered at night in prayer, to acknowledge what we are most grateful for.

There is a reason why we call those stories "special" and why they stay with our most trusted ones.

At the end of the day, I'm a wife to my husband and "furmom" to our boys, daughter to my parents, sibling to my sister, and an aunt to my niblings. Whatever I said or did earlier today shouldn't put shame on these roles, which I retire to everyday. If it does, I know in my heart that it's my mistake. Tomorrow, I need to do right by them again. This is how I keep my true north in my personal compass.

"Anywhere, anytime" —
Feels like home with you.
We can search this world for answers.
Perhaps, love.

Some people really take light from your flame. Don't ask them to stop. Pray for a wind of reasons to fan that flame and turn it into a wildfire.

This world we call ours deserves more light.

No day is ever perfect.
If we take time to celebrate a glimpse of that golden sunset;
If we stay mindful of oxygen in our lungs;
If we see people around us evolving to be better versions they never thought possible;
If we celebrate wins — some big, others small;
If we get to hug our loved ones at the end of the day,
It's a day we should not take for granted.
We can define the kind of day we live by the perspective we choose to keep.
Sometimes, our tanks may be short of stamina, but please, never of gratitude.

"It doesn't matter who's wrong,
It doesn't matter who's right,
But it matters that we forgive."

Anecdote: A snippet from my wedding vow; addressed to my husband.

In the eyes of the man I said "yes" to,
I switch between confidante and partner,
Yet every moment of silence shows that I am neither just one nor
the other.
I am the very core of who he needs, regardless of what that entails;
So much so that when he finds himself in a series of events, between
awesome and worrisome, he will always find his center — and he is
mine.

Sometimes, the best gift we can give ourselves is time. It's the one thing we can't be guilty of.

No age, position, or title grants anyone a courtroom to pass a verdict. Knowing something that someone else doesn't know doesn't give us any authority. It doesn't make us an expert.

The nobility of our intentions lies in our actions, which bring results and create unforgettable experiences for others — not in the stories we flaunt.

Woke up to this ray of sunshine. It's a hue almost reminiscent of sunset, yet it's the genesis of a new day.
First thought that came to mind?
Everything will be better soon.
To whoever is reading this and needing a reminder,
Hang in there.

No amount of apology or volumes of rationalized "whys" can ever, ever, EVER — bolster someone's ego.

Anything will escalate to an issue when you fight with a bruised ego. Even your slightest attempt to justify your words or actions will only inflate it. Do your world a favor —

Walk away.

Be with someone who will cause your heart to beat for reasons other than just to live.

One's definition of "better" or "worse" doesn't make it an absolute truth. One's personal standards do not define what others should adhere to. Respect is important when dealing with people's "preferences."

Do not assume you know exactly how the other person feels. Do not trample on their concerns either. Create a powerful shift from "I understand how you feel" to "I am sorry that's how you feel. Is there anything I can do?"

We don't know what others are going through. Social media may frame portions of our lives we want to showcase but they are never the entire story. When people post about how they're on travel revenge, appreciate what you can. When they share a new hobby or a milestone they're celebrating, does it bother you? People have the right to "choose their happy." Those others who bravely share their pains, heartbreaks, and sorrows either need an outlet to exhale or hope for support. Either way, people have different reasons for what they post, and those serve their own purpose, their business, or their current needs. It's a privilege to be given access to know about them and see them in their happiest or most vulnerable moments.

Amid all the seemingly "perfect," there is always a battle they're fighting or trying to survive. Either we help ease their pain or we scroll to the next post. Interpreting their reality doesn't make any of us the wiser, better or bigger person.

Remember moments that either made you gasp or took your breath away; those times that pinched nerves or tugged heartstrings; those chances that made you regret profoundly, or those you cheerfully celebrated. Every. Moment. Counts.

People will champion and celebrate you while there are others who will walk away; a majority will perhaps spectate. Through it all, learn to handpick those who lift you up when times get rough and those who wipe your tears or pull you up when you need them most.

The only validation we need is that of our hearts'. The only redemption we need is with those who love us unconditionally.

We don't need a gazillion people to feel validated when all our identity needs is authenticity. Our worth in this world doesn't take on its cloak of truth in what we have, what we wear, or what we can afford. Don't look for meaning where it doesn't exist. Sit in silence with the ones you love most and know that you're in the right place, holding their hand. That's the absolute and perfect intersection between what we need and what we deserve.

Some recent years were not easy. War broke whatever we had left of peace. Jobs may have been lost and the end of diseases unfound but even if we sum all the unpleasantries together, they will not come close to the reality that outweighs everything else today: We are here. We get to see another day of both good and bad. We get to choose. We get to do what we've been dreaming about a decade ago. That is a privilege, and the only currency that can afford gratitude.

Be grateful because today and for the next chapters of the book written about us, that happy ending doesn't change.

What is truly meant for us, will find us.
Everything that happened in our past will make sense.
Close the year, embrace the life that the new year brings. It just might be the year that saves us, and the very year that silences our fears and doubts.

The best of what's to come already has our name on it.
Do not relegate faith to a condition that requires "seeing it before believing it."

Priorities

Either you like it or you don't—
this pretty much describes
Matcha tea. It should be
served using 80℃ water and
becomes bitter as
temperature increases. It's
the preparation that also
makes it special requiring
targeted attention, just as
how your next musing will be
steeped in focus with this
question.

**If you were at an event where
you knew every guest, who
would be the first person you
would talk to?**

It is only in the dark when light shines brightest.
Do not feel uncomfortable with shining, but if it does get to you, choose to be that kind of light that is silently shared with others.

This way, there is no feeling of being alone, and the light that you cast is the only way for us to see others.

See how stars do not need to announce their coming and going, yet when one looks up at the sky on a moonless night, it's when their quiet is so loud. Their light, although not as bright as the moon or the sun, is enough to light the paths of those lost in the dark. It's shining just the same, sans the arrogance. It's neither too strong nor harmful. It's the kind of light that's just right. None of it is imposed or forced; hence, they rarely bother anyone.

Wouldn't it be nice to have this kind of presence to those around us?

Sunsets are meant to remind us that another day has ended but never without a beautiful purpose. It's the only "show" on earth that doesn't have a dire need to be noticed. It just does what it's meant to do.

If there's one thing you want to do without fear of being judged, what would that be?

The more we age (ergo, become wiser), the more we gravitate towards friendships that are easy. They're also the kind that gets the most mileage. They're friendships that don't demand anything more than showing up, and sharing food (and they drag stories that last longer than the meal itself). You binge-watch a flick or a TV series that appeals to your different personalities and strings interests together. You make the most random plans, not knowing sometimes when or where, but you know you will all show up.

Life doesn't always have to be difficult or complicated, and genuine friendships are about that — being there, even for no reason bigger than the spontaneity of it all.

Aspire to age gracefully with friends.
Don't pass judgment because of envy.
Don't downplay others' success or mock failure to create height for your own pedestal.
Don't patronize people because you need them.
Don't ignore others just because they can't augment your popularity.
Don't hate someone who hangs out with your enemy.
Don't engage in somebody else's battle.
Don't decide when you're mad or sad.
Don't forget those who pulled you up when you get to stand on top of the hill.
Don't promote prejudice against others' preferences just because they're different from yours.
Don't be someone you're not, in exchange for acknowledgment.
Don't cheat your way through the finish line just to settle a score.
Don't lie.
Don't pretend.
Don't gossip.
Don't condescend.
Just do good.

Don't ever make that foolish mistake or careless gesture of comparing your reality against someone else's social media feed.

Your mental health deserves better, and your heart will thank you for it.

We can't dance in the rain without getting drenched,
We can't reach the peak of a mountain without losing a breath,
In life, we can't filter the bad to gain the good;
But we get to choose what changes us.
Love and deal with heartbreaks, but move on.
Dream and take the pain of failure, but hope desperately.
Live your life and be ready to be judged, but remember, you don't
need to be validated.
Life will leave us with questions, sometimes with tears, even doubts,
but it's also guaranteed to leave you speechless; those moments will
make everything worth it.
Don't waste time residing in the unpleasantries.
Just take what's been arranged for you.
Share blessings.
Live unapologetically and be that person you're destined to be.

Same date, different year
Same promise, another cathedral
Among the constellations of stars that decide to sparkle or shy away
every night, I wake up every day, grateful that you are my sky.

Until you walk in the same shoes and cover the same steps as someone you judge with abundant posthaste, your words are empty, and make no mistake in seeing that they root from hollow maturity — juvenile nonetheless.

Remember that when we utter words of hate and angst, they speak so much of the person casting judgment, not the person being judged. That takes wisdom to see, humility to accept, and experience to be taught correctly.

Experience, as we know, is not something we inherit. Like respect, it is earned. A person without guilt can walk straight, even when the road is crooked.

Do not ever give someone the power to judge your journey. At the end of it all, you earn your steps while that person remains to be a spectator.

Be your own voice, not an echo.

Be the one to make a better stand, not swayed by age or position.

Be loyal to what's good, fair, and right, even if it means correcting someone you love.

Do not feel that the only way for you to score a point is to patronize. Values and principles should not be part of whatever generational wealth you are looking to inherit.

Wouldn't it be nice to find even a little crowd in a corner that respects you, rather than sing a viral tune on someone else's stage?

When we find ourselves on the brink of asking why, and the response is "why not," trust that it will be better than what we asked for.

Find your happy,
Be at peace with your resolve,
Don't use words to deflate others' sense of fun,
Take love and weaponize it to deal with indifference.
It would be nice to live in the honeymoon chapters of our lives,
It would be a privilege to make them last.

When we do things voluntarily, never prodded or demanded;
When we give our most precious time without any sense of
obligation but out of pure delight;
To be present;
To share your day's worth, but also to be heard without prejudice,
They speak of love.
When we do things to force copycat results;
When we pull out the white lies,
All the scheming unmasked with guilt traps,
That's manipulation.
A person who genuinely loves
Never manipulates.

People who do not value you for who you are,
For your authenticity and vulnerabilities altogether,
People who want to see you fail
Or those who want to be able to say they're right and you're wrong,
They do not deserve a seat at *your* table.
Don't let others dwarf your big heart.
Don't let them belittle your worth.
Your value doesn't diminish by someone else's opinion.
Don't give someone the power to judge especially if that person can't even take honest feedback.
Don't give them access to things that you love or people you care about.
Don't let them make a playground out of your affairs.
Live your life and fill it full, never bereft.
Someone will always say something,
The only checkpoint you do with yourself is to ask,
"Does that person matter to you anyway?"
Whether it's a yes or no,
That says it all,
Even what you do next.

Sometimes it's not about winning the race,
It's about finishing the long run.
Sometimes it's not about proving you're correct,
It's about being kind.
Sometimes it's not about showing off how much you know,
It's about knowing you helped someone without showing off.
Sometimes it's not about learning who betrayed you,
It's about not breaking someone else's trust.
The first lines make it easy to build a superficial reputation;
But the second lines define how we are remembered.
Fools parade and talk incessantly about themselves;
The wise let others speak of their greatness.
"Self-praise is no praise at all."

No matter how believable the story is,
If you've only listened to one side of it,
You only know half the story;
And the one who's very eager to tell you about it,
Is most likely the one who's out to defend a version that's farther
from the truth.

Personal Branding

Not only is Chamomile tea great for digestion, but it also improves cardiovascular health by reducing bad cholesterol. Due to the chemical compound *apigenin*, which is a flavonoid (a class of antioxidants), this tea is *associated* with sedative effects and promotes better sleep.

What is that one word that you want people to associate you with?

Some of us close our eyes to dream.
A few lucky ones wake up to it. Everyday.
Don't put off whatever brings us closer to our dreams.
Let's live our lives in such a way that our dreams are something we appreciate — wide awake.

Live your life in a way that inspires others to live theirs authentically,
happily in their own state, and not as a replica of yours.
Do not envy others for what they have,
Do not hold high regard for what they achieve,
Do not succumb to their superficial "shows."
You were not given their lives because you were meant to live better.

When we weaponize hate to stain someone else's character, trust that you'll get hit by a ricochet of karma. This comes at a high price because peace of mind is what you auction off, and it is in a currency you can't afford to recover.

Even if you think you have the ability and authority to talk down on someone and be condescending, people may be "forced" to do it your way. However, trust that it will not bring you genuine happiness because nothing you get is done out of love.

Our words can uplift sunken hopes; energize a tired soul. Their effects are unmistakable on someone who needs to hear them at the right time. Sadly, our words can also deflate someone else's spirit or totally wreck someone's disposition when abused or spoken without careful thought. Its repercussions are damaging and destructive, or worse, they can leave someone broken. Equivocal to timing, our choice of words and tone play substantial roles in protecting the integrity of our intentions.

I learned though, that no amount of caution can protect our purpose (even when coupled with all the care in our hearts) if the recipient is too arrogant to change. Similarly, no amount of blatant and brutal honesty can break a person who desires to be better each day. Authenticity prevails when you can speak in exactly the same manner and use exactly the same words to someone as you would, while you have an audience at a listening distance.

I also learned that there is always a better flow of communication when we free ourselves from a mindset rotten by hierarchy or superiority complex, or when we intend to listen more than react. We learn so much from our seniors, who speak to inspire, without authority in their heads, and who are able to listen without prejudice. We run away from those who, by their words and actions, just want to feed their ego or throw weight around because they think they have to be in control. We cannot change the world with one sentence, but sometimes, what we say means the whole world to someone.

Can you relate to that feeling when you simply look forward to talking to someone? What a world of difference it makes if we all attempt to be — somebody for someone.

"Culture is what people do when no one is watching."

Meanwhile, character is what someone reveals when there is no audience to impress. It unveils itself, especially during most extreme circumstances. This is why we hear the phrase, "a true test of character."

People love to put up a show. "Human nature" tips the scale in favor of its feeble existence. Character defines who we really are when the curtains are down and we think no one is looking.

While we belong to a certain "culture," we are fully and solely accountable for our character.

"She thinks she's *always* right."
Such is the shortest and saddest story of a narcissist.

When we lose someone, it opens a gateway of regrets:
Of seconds we spent nagging rather than loving,
Of minutes we wasted doing verbal diarrhea, taking every account
of mistake and misunderstanding rather than listening,
Of hours burned assuming rather than asking,
Of days feeding our ego instead of understanding,
Of months leaving that other person broken, judged, and exposed,
Of forcing them to live in the image of your shadow rather than
carrying their own light,
Of a lifetime of your prejudice rather than acceptance.
Don't let that day be the only time we realize how wrong we are
because sometimes, today is all we have.

One of the harshest outcomes out there is when you try to change someone by crucifying him to your own imposed crosses; grudges overspilling into conversations, only to remind that person why he "changed" in the first place.

The most painful outcome though is to know the reason all along was you.

Sometimes it's easy to forgive others,
But it takes a tremendous amount of humility to forgive ourselves.
As such, we end up "forgiving"
But not moving on.
It may be easy to fool others in plain sight,
But the inner struggle will break every inch of our sanity — and
that's the kind of rut that's hard to emancipate from.
There is no peace of mind,
When there is no forgiveness.
The dissonance would be loud enough that we wouldn't even be
able to hear our own heartbeat —
And love is forgotten.
If there is no more forgiveness, there is no love.

In our personal relationships, people behave differently because they're either hurt, conflicted, or struggling with something or someone.

However, when a relationship becomes toxic, people leave. The nasty truth is, we sometimes worry so hard about our reputation that we actually forget to build and nourish relationships.

Every day, we get to decide what we trade off.

The truth doesn't reside in the lips.
It doesn't take up temporary space where it is convenient, where
there is selective audience, or where it aims to just serve the agenda
of the speaker.

Deep down in our hearts, truth cannot be muted.
It is only with absolute honesty that it finds ears,
And the resolve to change circumstances.
Even in silence, truth is heard.
The person who speaks and screams loudest is not always,
truthfully, the victim.
Before we cast judgment on anyone we accuse of hurting us, take a
humble moment to ask,

What have we done?

An honest story is one that is not stained by omission.
A heart that knows the truth, is either set free —
Or it continues to carry the burden.

Everyone deals with some kind of stigma.
An annulled husband hoping for a better partner;
A single parent trying to make ends meet for her three kids;
A female executive who's trying to do good by everyone despite gender discrimination;
A freelance travel agent who lost his business during the pandemic;
A daughter who can't reveal her own true identity because of a controlling parent;
A superstar who's gone through several divorces;
There is stigma because there is judgment.

Imagine a world where people do not have to live according to how society conventionally sees these circumstances.

Imagine a world where the only requirements for every human being are to live well and to not harm others (in whatever humanly possible way).

A stigma would cease to exist when one nips judgment in the bud or wears an armor of indifference.

Let's live our lives with ardent desire to free our mental disposition from chains imposed by judgment.

Legacy

White tea is made from the youngest leaves and buds of the plant. It is said to minimize wrinkles. Let this tea pique your thoughts around life and aging.

If you were to have a biography, what would be its title?

Not everyone is as strong as you are,
Someone may just be coming out of a painful loss that you didn't
know about.
Treat people with care.

Not everyone can afford what you have,
Someone might be feeding his family leftovers without guarantee of
food or water the next day.
Be grateful for what you have; be generous with what you share.

Not everyone has access to your knowledge,
It doesn't mean you know better or that you're wiser,
Or that you have the power to be condescending.
Nobody knows everything, and as such, we are all short of
something.

We can argue the whole day about who's wrong or right but the person we all remember is the one who chose to forgive.

Each of us has a myriad of dreams, and we make a lifetime of eventful choices about what and who gets to be part of them. The story is yours and you get full say on who you acclaim to be the protagonists of every chapter in that plot.

Don't let others tell you to wait and take the back seat, especially when it's about fighting for your dreams and securing nothing less than centerstage.

Do what you have to do. If your intention is good, learn not to be bothered by what others think. Live without regret that you did what you did because you cared. If that merits a positive outcome, smile quietly and inspire others to do the same. If you are received inimically, just move on. Good intentions don't need explanation, and you don't owe anyone the same. Others will even conspire to upset you. Don't give them the pleasure of seeing you rankled. This is what you remind yourself when they throw you off guard:

"The only opinion that should matter belongs to people you care about. Don't mind those who don't matter."

Put it up as your shield, and keep firing the universe with positive intentions anyway. Select your battles and march on to help others who are willing to be helped. Others who think of you negatively will find their places in this world. Trust me. People will talk behind your back, but nothing changes the fact that they remain behind you, and that puts you in the lead. Some will agitate you by showing less amount of care. It should not change how much you are capable of giving anyway, and believe me, there will be others who are willing recipients of that much effort — and will thank you for it.

Your happiness is your business.

Embrace the fact that your choice is not for everyone to understand. Walk away from people who doubt what you can do in this world. Don't ever be limited by what they say.

Your best revenge is to let them watch you live your life exceeding the very limits of their opinion of you.

When they expect you to fail, you soar high.

Don't expect others to "consider the consequences" of their actions when you failed to practice what you proclaimed to preach.

You are meant to do more than what people expect you to do. However, if you keep allowing others to define your limitations, you're giving up your full potential.

Don't give them the right to box you in a cubicle when you're meant to get the corner office.
Don't give them the power to call you names when you don't deserve anything less than a proper noun.
Don't let the majority dictate what you can accomplish.
Don't give them the convenience of sizing you up based on your gender.
People always have their agenda.
Don't waste your time serving any other purpose than becoming relevant and essential.

If anyone calls your A-game "drama" simply because you're a woman, put out the best results no one has ever achieved before — and in your brightest red lippie (red stilettos will work, too!)

You're the star of your story and those making "noise" do not own the show.

Don't let them change the narrative.

Beware of leaders who will camouflage their inability to decide or take action and hide them under the guise of "empowerment." The general idea of being trusted should come with a feeling of recognition, not delegation.

May we not experience loss before we learn to value someone.
May we not be at the mercy of forgiveness before we rid ourselves
of ego.
May we not find ourselves destitute of time before we decide who
is important to us.
May we not have to utter the words "if only I knew" before we end
a relationship out of petulance.
May we not get stuck at a dead end of regret before we put off
another chance that we have — not knowing it's the last one.

You stabbed my heart like an encore performance when I haven't even recovered from the clot you caused when you ended things with me — to be with him.

Mischievous fate had it though: that my song has always been with someone who came later in life, albeit "late" by definition in my prematurely impatient timeline. Wisdom finally orchestrated a show I never thought I deserved, and it turned out to be "just in time."

Trust that there's always a better beginning. You just have to let go of something that is not yours, that is not good for you, that has to end.

When the man of the moment gives you the time of day, no woman
ever thinks that he's *not* the one.

Every message or gesture, in every moment: they all become fibers
entwined in an emotional fabric that gives us that warm and fuzzy
feeling. We create that bed for ourselves, not wanting to wake up
to a morning that is different from the evening that was.

Sometimes, though, once we have finally woken up, all the make-
believe ends, and the painful truth begins —
While he treated you as a pawn
You crowned him your king.

Why does forgiveness hurt?
Because at one point, perhaps several for others, a piece of your heart was taken from you and somehow, in forgiving, you have to give more of it away.

Why does it give you relief even when it hurts?
Because the act of forgiving is always by choice, one that is given with humility and kindness. When we give more, we are reminded of our full capacity to understand. Despite that sense of loss, we become a bigger person when we forgive. It leaves you with that feeling that we actually gain more than what we initially lost.

Only love does that.

You cannot forgive when there is no love.
So when we find it difficult to forgive, we should ask ourselves, "How much do I love this person?"

Why does it seem that when we say, "I will forgive, but I cannot forget," it doesn't work exactly the same way? Because when we for*give*, it only becomes more powerful when we for*get* the pain. While we give more of our hearts away, we also get something back.

That is peace of mind.

Don't let the weight of our ego block the very space where peace of mind deserves to take permanent residence.

It's the light we carry that makes the place shimmer.
Don't let anyone put out that light.
Don't feel threatened by others sparkling on their own.
It becomes a brighter world when we outshine the dark, together.

Get

What you

Want

(Now, read that again but start from the bottom.)
Which one is your mantra?

Time

Unlike the Roobois tea, which doesn't taste bitter even when over-steeped, this question is at the mercy of time. It is supposed to bring a memory back to life. Hopefully, it quells a "what if" that had been brewing with us subconsciously or satiates an intense longing for someone you lost.

What moment in the past would you choose to relive or recreate with someone you loved immensely, but lost because you were out of time?

Acknowledgments

I am literally pinching myself after I punctuate the last sentence of this page. I really did not think and plan for this book to take physical form at this stage in my life. In my vision board, I manifested that I would be documenting my musings during a retreat of some sort, detached from my current realities. I guess a pandemic, a war in Gaza, and other current events have somehow put pressure on the fast-forward button of my timeline. I did claim that this "what if" would then be eclipsed by a byline like a sequel to that Young Blood article I wrote and published by the Philippine Daily Inquirer many years ago. Holidays turned into working days, and weekends were deprived of my usual mallrat routine, which all surprisingly turned out to be better for me and my pockets. I had most of these musings from the archives of my social media accounts, so it only took a couple of weekends to consolidate them into one file, and voila — the majority of the content was already available. I don't think my noggin would have both the capacities and creatives to muster up crafting fictional stories, but reflections are absolutely my cup of tea. Then the whole idea of question-and-tea pairings surfaced like an epiphany of sorts because I didn't think it was also socially normal to sip soup all day.

I thank both readers and likers of my posts, who also served as catalysts to the idea of publishing this collection. I am grateful for those random messages even from people I didn't know from Adam who said my thoughts helped them navigate through an episode that they were going through or from friends who stayed engaged through verbose posts and even encouraged me to "write my own book." To those of you who propelled what used to be just an idea to what is now a book, thank you for believing in me.

I want to express my profuse thanks to my husband, Alvin, for fully supporting me in this endeavor. He has always been my champion in the idea of publishing a book, so to us both, this was just really a matter of "when." He knew even from the start that this was something I was determined to do in my lifetime, so when I made my claim that 2024 is the year we would publish, he said, "Go for it!" He repeated those words every time he sensed some challenges that either derailed or discouraged me. This section is shared with our boys: his Royal Littleness Pepper and his Royal Cuteness Almond, who are the real VIPs in our household.

To my parents, Nanay and Tatay, thank you for inspiring me sufficiently enough to re-tell some stories that tugged my own heartstrings. Thank you for endlessly showing us unconditional love, even during days when we didn't deserve it. Most of all, thank you for your daily prayers that powerfully dwarf anxieties or fears, and bridge the distance from Antipolo mountains to McKinley Hill. You have absolutely made it possible to allow us, your daughters, to be in our own skin and excel in our own unique ways - individually or together. Thank you for raising us out of love and not authority; to follow (and even concede) out of respect but never fear. Thank you for living your lives with overflowing kindness that no self-praise is necessary to orchestrate a show. People normally love to talk about their accomplishments and rarely give credit where it is due. In this book, allow me to give it all back to you. You are both the very reason why I exist, and you are both my inspiration and why I aspire to always be better. Your selflessness took almost no credit, and you even gave whatever little was left to add to our love tanks that are now bigger than we ever hoped them to be; big enough to power us through hurdles, heartbreaks, and life's disappointments. Our family receives the biggest boons for every single day that you both continue to live. Thank you to my sister, Ate Maco, for being a source of real courage fighting the Big C, even when remission and medicines hurt so bad. You are always the quiet one - but in that serenity lies your strength.

To my niblings, Paolo, Mai, and Marco — thank you for being my pilot critics. With your honest and candid feedback on my book's concept to those page breakers that went through several iterations, I mean it when I say that I pale to insignificance next to your brilliance. I am perpetually privileged to have been branded as the "cool tita" (next to your cool Tito Alvin). We may have chosen a marital path without kids - but boy, oh boy, we did hit the lottery with you, three! You have no idea how much we gush over your achievements (but those surprise food treats hopefully send the right messages). Special shout out to Marco for putting a "face" to this book.

Thank you to Don Jaucian for agreeing to be my editor despite my being a "noob" (yes, "newbie") in the immersive world of writing. I hope you continue to accept more editorial stints and help other inveterate writers like yours truly. Our connection was established through a good friend, O (Oliver), who I also look up to in both the publishing industry and the world of the arts. Special thanks to "Kaps" (Sherwin) for "stirring" my own thoughts until I finally managed to concretize the book title.

To all my friends, who have been at the mercy of pseudonyms I invented for endearment: those I call "sisters, brothers," or even "twins," and those I call by the first letter of their names — you all know who you are. I may have been raised by our parents well enough to fit well in societies of varying natures, but thank you for keying in your influences even harder enough to activate my misfits — only in a good way. You all have been part of these musings, as patient listeners to the litany of things I had to ramble about or even as guilty sponsors, co-hosts, or overindulging besties who knew that as soon as musings started to flow, so did the bottles of wine, and kettles of tea or coffee with whatever space is left for cake. Thank you for being on my side of "crazy," and thanks for sharing all those meals with me because I can't imagine how my hips would have turned out if I ate them all by myself. There were times when my thoughts were not as clear as my green tea, so thank you for enduring my "matcha" moments.

Last but not the least - to you, whoever you are, who traded off an afternoon tea with a friend for some hours of solitude hoping to find inspiration (or answers) in this book, know that you may have just jump-started your own journey to getting "lost in your own thoughts."

Worry not, for no search parties will be sent.

Another cup of tea, perhaps?

ABOUT THE AUTHOR

Thea Panes-Demetillo is a random muser until her thoughts found their way to online platforms which helped her evolve into a self-branded inveterate writer. Her true north has always been travel but her career's trajectory has led her to off-the-beaten paths of Business Operations, Sales, Finance, Business Partners Management, Learning and Business Transformation. She is a modern day storyteller by choice.

She is married to Alvin Demetillo, and together they share "paw-rental" love and cuddles with their dogs — Pepper and Almond. Although born and based in the Philippines, she considers herself being "raised by the world" having visited 49 countries (as of this publication).

Musing sobriety doesn't exist in her world.